LEE HOIBY

BERMUDAS

Vocal Duet and Piano

ED-3832
First Printing: June 1993

G. SCHIRMER, Inc.

Distributed by
Hal Leonard Publishing Corporation
7777 West Bluemound Road P.O. Box 13819 Milwaukee, WI 53213

In 1653 Andrew Marvell was tutor to the ward of Oliver Cromwell, the Lord Protector of England. Marvell lived in an atmosphere of social, economic, and religious ferment in the home of John Oxenbridge, one of the Puritans who had fled England to escape religious persecution, like the Massachusetts colonists of the Mayflower. For several years Oxenbridge had been the leader of a pilgrim settlement on the remote Caribbean islands named the Bermudas, after the Spaniard Bermudez, who discovered them in 1515. When Cromwell's "glorious revolution" triumphed Oxenbridge returned to England and served on the London Commission for the Government of the Bermudas. These islands were widely believed to be bewitched, the subject of lurid legends and tall tales which are the source of today's Bermuda Triangle stories. In *The Tempest,* Shakespeare had invoked them as "still-vex'd [that is, ever stormy] Bermoothes," a typically erroneous description, as any vacationer can now attest. Oxenbridge was in charge of the sale of shares in a company organized to exploit the island at the time that his young poet-in-residence composed these balmy lines.

Marvell's elegant poem dispels the fantastic tales that were plaguing the island's reputation and inhibiting investors. It replaces them with an accurate list of Bermuda's resources, couched in language drawn from the Psalms of David and the Song of Solomon, in keeping with the high spiritual tone of Cromwell's Puritan regime. It evokes the buoyant faith of the hymning pilgrims for whom the tropical wonders are emblems of divinity. The seeming naivete of the poem, however, is artful. Marvell was perfectly aware that a large cache of valuable "Ambergris on shoar" had provoked the island's first recorded crime; that for some the "Gospels pearl" was no consolation for the disappointingly small oyster's pearl; and that safety from "the Prelat's rage" had quickly given way to doctrinal violence. But *Bermudas* is no less a charming devotional masterpiece for being a remarkable stock prospectus as well. It blithely transcends politics and economics to employ the island as a metaphor for the blessings to be conferred upon the faithful.

—MARK SHULGASSER

duration: ca. 8 minutes

Bermudas is also available in a version for middle voice and piano, order no. 50481991

Both versions may be performed with piano quartet accompaniment.

Performance material is available on rental from the publisher.

Bermudas

Where the remote *Bermudas* ride
In th' Oceans bosome unespy'd,
From a small Boat, that row'd along,
The listning Winds receiv'd this Song.
   What should we do but sing his Praise
That led us through the watry Maze,
Unto an Isle so long unknown,
And yet far kinder than our own?
Where he the huge Sea-Monsters wracks,
That lift the Deep upon their Backs.
He lands us on a grassy Stage;
Safe from the Storms, and Prelat's rage.
He gave us this eternal Spring,
Which here enamells every thing;
And sends the Fowl's to us in care,
On daily Visits through the Air.
He hangs in shades the Orange bright,
Like golden Lamps in a green Night.
*[And does in the Pomgranates close,
Jewels more rich than *Ormus* show's]
He makes the Figs our mouths to meet;
And throws the Melons at our feet.
But Apples plants of such a price,
No Tree could ever bear them twice.
With Cedars, chosen by his hand,
From *Lebanon,* he stores the Land.
And makes the hollow Seas, that roar,
Proclaime the Ambergris on shoar.
He cast (of which we rather boast)
The Gospels Pearl upon our Coast.
And in these Rocks for us did frame
A Temple, where to sound his Name.
Oh let our Voice his Praise exalt,
Till it arrive at Heavens Vault:
Which thence (perhaps) rebounding, may
Eccho beyond the *Mexique Bay.*
Thus sung they, in the *English* boat,
An holy and a chearful Note,
And all the way, to guide their Chime,
With falling Oars they kept the time.

—ANDREW MARVELL, 1621–78

* The two lines enclosed in brackets are not set to music.

for Katherine and Kristine Ciesinski

BERMUDAS

Andrew Marvell

Lee Hoiby, Op. 37

un - es - py'd,

From a small Boat, that row'd a - long,

The list - 'ning Waves re -

ceived this song.

Allegretto ♩ = 100

far kind - er than our own?

Where he the huge Sea - Mon - sters wracks,

Where he the huge Sea - Mon - sters wracks,

That lift the Deep ___ up-on their Backs.   He

That lift the Deep ___ up-on their Backs.   He

lands _____ us on a grass-y Stage; _____ Safe from the

lands _____ us on a grass-y Stage; _____ Safe from the

f

dim.

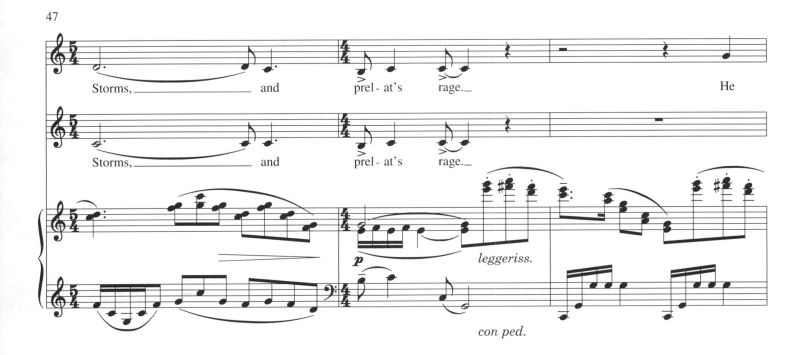

Storms, _____ and prel-at's rage.____ He

Storms, _____ and prel-at's rage.____

p   *leggeriss.*

con ped.

Gave us this e-ter-nal Spring, Which here e-nam-els

ev - 'ry - thing;

And sends the Fowls to us in

care _____ On dai - ly Vis - its through the air.

He hangs in shades the Or - ange bright, Like

He hangs in shades the Or - ange bright,

61 *largamente* ... *ritard.*

gold - - en Lamps in a green

Like gold - - en Lamps in a green

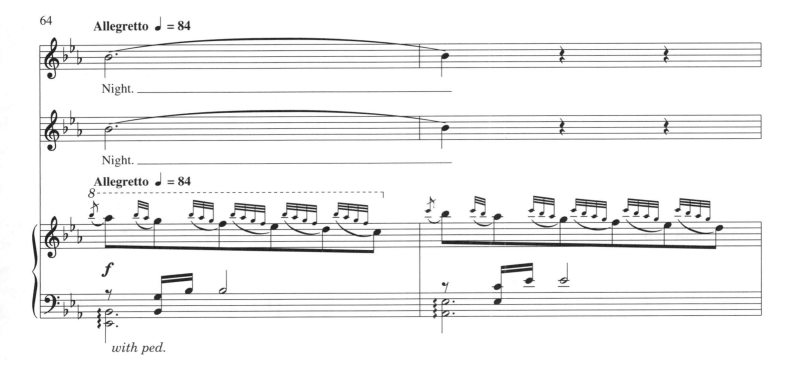

64 **Allegretto** ♩ = 84

Night. _____

Night. _____

with ped.

66

He

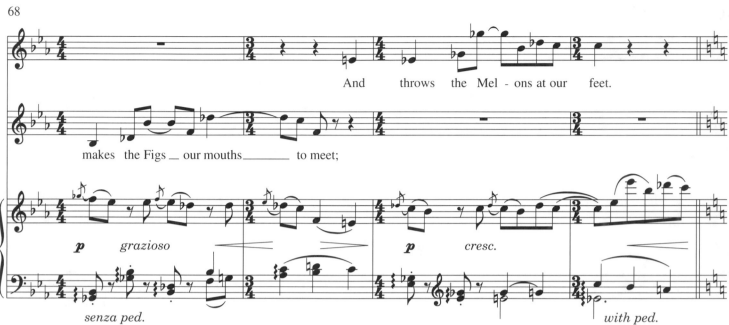

And throws the Mel - ons at our feet.

makes the Figs __ our mouths _____ to meet;

p *grazioso* *p* *cresc.*

senza ped. *with ped.*

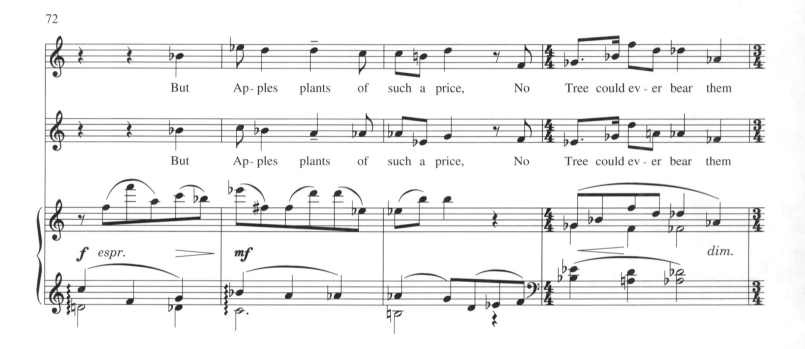

But Ap- ples plants of such a price, No Tree could ev - er bear them

But Ap- ples plants of such a price, No Tree could ev - er bear them

f *espr.* *mf* *dim.*

ritard.

twice. With Ce - dars cho- sen by his hand, From

ritard.

twice. With Ce - dars cho- sen by his hand, From

legato *ritard.* *mf*

3 *3* *3*

pp

with ped.

80

a tempo   *allargando*

Leb - a - non   he   stores _____ the   Land. _____

a tempo   *allargando*

Leb - a - non   he   stores _____ the   Land. _____

cresc. ed allargando

a tempo

83   **Allegro** ♩ = 112

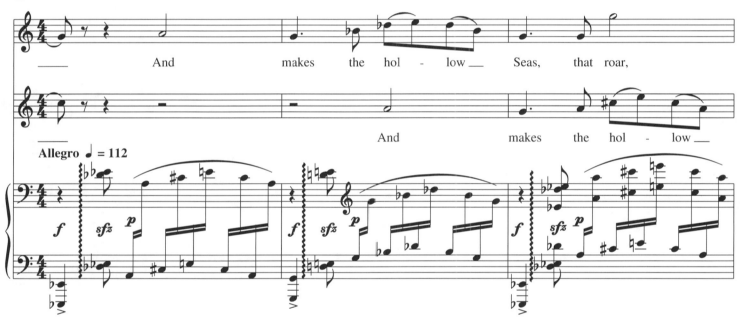

___ And   makes   the   hol - low ___ Seas,   that   roar,

And   makes   the   hol - low ___

Allegro ♩ = 112

86

Pro - claime   the   Am - - - - ber - gris   on

Seas,   that   roar,   Pro - claime the   Am - - ber - gris   on

Shoar.

108

poco a poco animando

Name. Oh let our Voice his Praise ex -

poco a poco animando

Name. Oh _____ let our Voice his Praise ex -

poco a poco animando

112 ♩ = 88

alt, _____ Til it ar - rive at Heav - ens

alt, _____ Til it ar - rive at Heav - ens

♩ = 88

f

p

114 *poco ritard.* *a tempo, marcato*

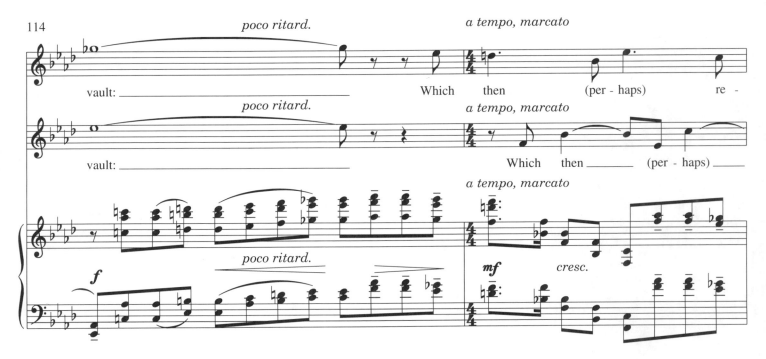

vault: _____ Which then (per - haps) re -

poco ritard. *a tempo, marcato*

vault: _____ Which then _____ (per - haps) _____

a tempo, marcato

poco ritard.

f *mf* *cresc.*

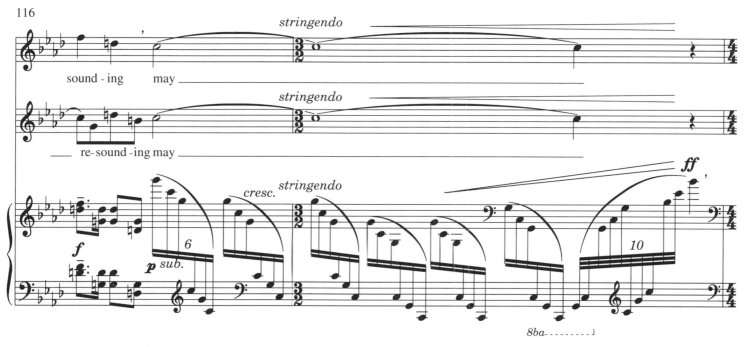

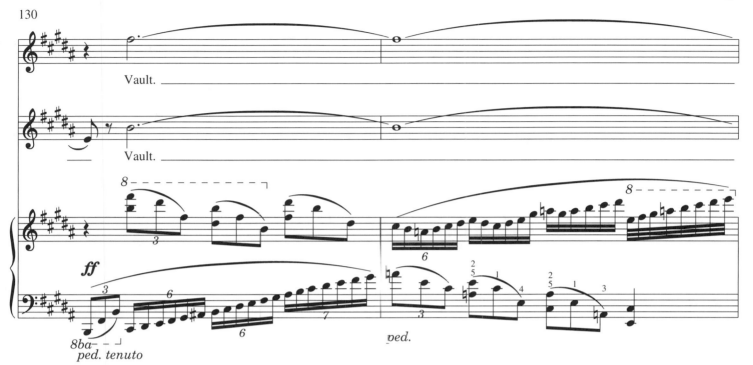

they in the Eng - lish Boat, A

ho - - ly and a cheer - ful Note, And

all the way, to guide their Chime,

With fall - - ing Oars they kept the

time.

diminuendo

poco ritard.

sempre dim.

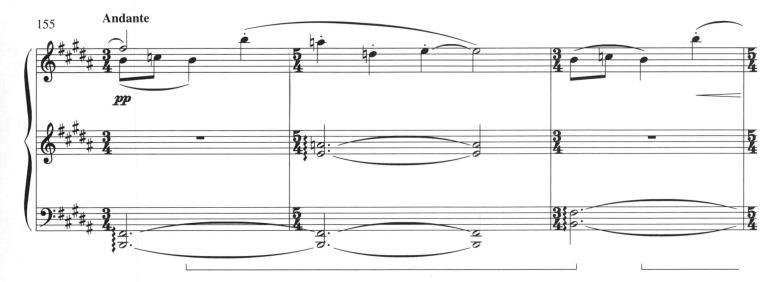

Andante

pp

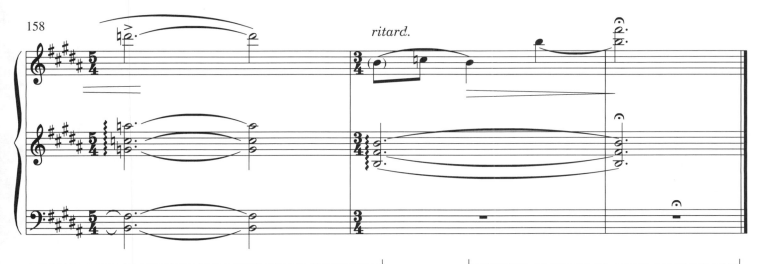

ritard.